The Kindness of Strangers

I Talk You Talk Press

CONTENTS

I Talk You Talk Press

1. THE WOMAN IN THE SUPERMARKET

Jenny was in the supermarket. She was with her son, Daniel. He was four years old. The supermarket was very busy. It was 6:00pm. Jenny finished work at 5:00pm. She picked up Daniel from the kindergarten. Then, she went to the supermarket.

"I want candy!" said Daniel. "I want candy! I want candy!"

"Be quiet," said Jenny. "I will get you some candy, but first, I have to buy food for dinner tonight."

"I want candy! I want candy now!" shouted Daniel.

"Wait! And please be quiet!" said Jenny.

Jenny went to the vegetable section and picked up some potatoes, carrots, onions and broccoli. She planned to make stew. It was winter, and she wanted to eat something warm. Then, she went to the milk section and picked up some milk. She bought some yoghurts for breakfast.

I have chicken for the stew at home. But I need bread, she thought.

She went to the bakery section. Daniel saw the cakes.

"I want cake! I want cake!" he shouted. People looked at him.

"Be quiet Daniel! I'll buy you some candy, but you can't have cake too!" said Jenny.

"But I want chocolate cake!" shouted Daniel.

I want to get out of here quickly, thought Jenny. She picked up some bread and put it in her shopping basket.

"I want that chocolate cake!" shouted Daniel. He started to cry.

Jenny walked to the juice section and got some orange juice.

"Now, we can go to the candy section," said Jenny.

"Yes!" said Daniel. He stopped crying and smiled.

They walked to the candy section.

"OK, you can choose one item," said Jenny. "Be quick."

Daniel looked at all the candy. Then, he chose a bag of chocolate.

"Do you want this?" asked Jenny. "OK, put it in the basket."

Daniel put it in the basket.

"OK, we are finished. Let's go to the checkout," said Jenny.

They walked through the supermarket to the checkout. There were long lines at all the checkout desks.

Oh no! thought Jenny. *There are so many people!*

Jenny and Daniel got in line. After ten minutes, Daniel was tired.

"I don't want to stand here!" he said. "I want to go!"

"We can't go. We have to pay for our shopping. We have to wait," said Jenny.

"I want my candy now!" said Daniel.

"You have to wait! We have to pay first!" said Jenny.

The line moved slowly. The people in front of Jenny had a lot of items.

After twenty minutes, Jenny and Daniel reached the checkout desk. Jenny put her shopping on the desk.

"Hello!" said the cashier.

"Hello," said Jenny.

The cashier scanned all of Jenny's items. Jenny put the items into a large bag.

"I want my candy!" shouted Daniel.

Jenny gave Daniel the candy. He opened it and started to eat it.

"That's thirty pounds and fifty-two pence please," said the cashier.

Jenny took out her credit card and put it into the credit card machine. Then she waited. Something was wrong. The machine didn't accept the card.

There was a long line of people behind Jenny. They were all looking at her.

"I'm sorry, you can't use this card. Do you have another card? Or cash?" asked the cashier.

"Jenny looked in her purse. "Oh no! I don't have any cash! I didn't have time to go to the bank today. And I don't have another card!"

"Well, I'm sorry, but you can't buy these items," said the cashier.

Jenny looked at Daniel. He was eating the chocolate.

"Oh no," said Jenny. "I'm sorry. My son is already eating the chocolate."

Jenny covered her face with her hands. "I'll put the items back," she said. "Can I pay for the chocolate tomorrow?"

"I need to talk to my manager," said the cashier.

"Excuse me."

The cashier and Jenny looked at the woman behind Jenny. She was a few years older than Jenny.

Oh no, thought Jenny. *She is going to get angry with me. I am taking too much time, and everyone is waiting.*

"Here is my credit card," said the woman. "I'll pay for your items."

"What? No, it's OK," said Jenny. She was very shocked.

"I don't mind," said the woman. She gave the cashier a credit card. "Put it on my card."

"OK," said the cashier.

Jenny looked at the woman. She started to cry.

"Thank you so much," she said. "Thank you. Today was a really busy day, and my son is very noisy. You are so kind."

"It's OK," said the woman, smiling. "I like to do nice things for other people."

The cashier gave the card back to the woman.

Jenny picked up her bag and held Daniel's hand. "Thank you so much," she said again. "I won't forget this. If I see someone who needs help, I will help them."

The woman smiled. "You are welcome. Now go home and cook dinner for your son!"

2. CHRISTMAS KINDNESS

It was Christmas morning. Annette was excited. She was nine years old. She woke up at 6:30am. She wanted to go downstairs and open her presents. She walked into her parents' bedroom. Her parents were asleep.

"Merry Christmas!" she shouted.

Her mother and father woke up. "Merry Christmas, Annette," said her father. "What time is it?"

"It's six thirty. Can I open my presents?"

"Wait for me and your mother to get up," said her father. "Wait in your room. We will get up now."

Annette went back into her room and looked out of the window.

That's strange, she thought. *There is a police car outside the house across the road.*

Annette didn't know the people in the house across the road. They were new neighbours. They moved into the house only a month ago. They had a daughter, who was about seven years old. Annette's parents spoke to the family when they moved into the street, but Annette didn't. She was at school that day.

Why is there a police car outside their house on Christmas Day? she thought.

Annette's mother and father came into her bedroom.

"Mom, Dad, there is a police car outside the house across the road. Look," she said. Her mother and father looked out of the window.

"What's happened?" asked her mother.

"I don't know, but we should go and see. Maybe something bad has happened. Annette, wait here. Don't go into the living room and open your presents yet. Wait until we come back," said Annette's father.

"OK," said Annette. She sat on her bed and looked out of the window. She watched her mother and father go across the road and knock on the door of the house. A policewoman opened the door. The family in the house came to the door too. They spoke for a while.

The little girl is crying, thought Annette. *What has happened?*

About ten minutes later, Annette's mother and father came back. Annette went down the stairs and met her parents in the hall.

"What happened?" she asked.

"It's terrible," said her mother. "Last night, a bad person broke into the house and took all the little girl's presents."

"Took her presents?" asked Annette. "That's terrible! Santa brought her presents, and then someone took them! Who took them?"

"The police don't know," said her father. "They are trying to get information."

Annette felt sad. Christmas was a happy time, but she was thinking about the young girl. Her Christmas was very bad.

"Can I go into the living room now and look at my presents?" she asked.

"Yes, let's go into the living room. Let's see if Santa came to our house last night," said Annette's mother.

Annette opened the living room door. "Santa came last night!" she shouted. "There are so many presents!" She looked around the living room. There were presents everywhere. They were under the Christmas tree, on the floor and on the sofa.

"Open your presents," said Annette's father.

Annette didn't move.

"What's wrong?" asked Annette's mother.

"That girl across the road. She has no presents to open," said Annette. "I'm going to give her some of my presents."

Annette's mother and father looked at each other.

"Annette, that is very kind of you," said her mother.

"Help me carry them across the road," said Annette. She picked up some presents. Her mother and father picked up some presents too.

They carried the presents out of the house and across the road.

Annette's mother rang the bell. The little girl and her mother came to the door.

"Merry Christmas!" said Annette. "These presents are for you!"

The little girl looked at Annette and then looked at her mother.

"What? No, you can't. Oh, this is so kind of you!" said the girl's mother. She started to cry. The little girl stopped crying.

"Are they for me?" she asked quietly.

"Yes! They are for you!" said Annette.

"Come in," said the girl's mother.

Annette and her mother and father walked into the house. They went into the living room. The policewoman was talking to the girl's father.

"The nice family from across the road have brought some presents for Suzy," said the girl's mother.

"Oh, that's so nice!" said Suzy's father and the policewoman.

Annette and her mother and father put the presents under the Christmas tree.

"Open them!" said Annette.

Suzy walked over to the presents. She picked up a box and unwrapped it.

"Oh, a doll! It's so pretty!" she said. She smiled. She looked at Annette. "Thank you! You are my new best friend!"

Annette smiled. "Let's be friends. Come to my house later. We can play with our new toys together!"

3. THE ARTIST ON THE TRAIN

Marty was an artist. He was good at drawing many things. When he went out, he always took his sketchbook and pencils with him. He sat in parks and drew the trees and flowers. He sat outside cafes and drew the streets. He posted his pictures on Instagram. He had about five hundred followers.

Marty worked in a bakery. He wanted to become a professional artist, but it was difficult. He needed money. So, he worked in the bakery to get money, and posted his drawings on Instagram to try to get some fans.

One day, Marty was on the train. He was going to work. A woman was sitting opposite him. She had long brown hair and was wearing a thick black coat. She was about 30 years old. She was looking at her phone. She didn't look at Marty.

I'd like to do something nice for someone today, thought Marty. *I'd like to draw her.*

He took out his sketchbook and pencils, and started to draw. The train moved a lot, so it was difficult to draw well, but Marty was a very good artist. He started to draw the woman's face and hair, and then her shoulders. He looked at her for a few seconds, and then drew a few lines. Then, he looked at her for a few more seconds, and then drew a few more lines. Soon, the picture looked like the woman. The train slowed down.

I hope she doesn't get off the train here, thought Marty. The woman didn't move.

Good. She is probably going to the same station as me.

Marty took some coloured pencils out of his bag and added a little colour. He added brown to her hair, and some gold to her earrings.

A man was sitting next to him. He looked at the drawing.

"That's excellent," he said quietly. "It looks like a photograph."

"Thanks," said Marty.

Marty added a little more colour to the picture, and then it was finished. The train slowed down. Marty and the woman stood up.

"Excuse me," said Marty.

The woman looked at him. "Yes?"

"I hope you don't mind, but I drew a picture of you. Here, you can keep it."

Marty gave the picture to the woman.

"Ahh!" The woman was very surprised. She looked at the picture, then she looked at Marty. She started to cry.

"This is so nice!" she said. "No one has ever done something so nice to me before! Thank you!"

Marty smiled. "You're welcome."

"Can I really keep it?" she asked.

"Of course," said Marty.

The train stopped and they got off the train.

"Can I ask your name?" asked the woman.

"Marty Jones," said Marty.

Thank you so much, Marty," said the woman. Marty smiled and walked away.

The next day, Marty opened his Instagram account and looked at the number of followers. He was shocked. He had four thousand new followers!

What? Why do I have so many followers? he thought. Then he saw a message. He opened up the message and read it.

---Dear Marty, I wanted to say thank you again for drawing the picture of me on the train yesterday. I am a photographer, and I have many followers on Instagram. I posted the picture of me and the story about you on my Instagram page. Many people were interested in your story. I told them to follow you. I hope you don't mind. From Charlotte.---

There was another message. Marty opened it and read it.

---Dear Marty, I am an editor for a magazine. I saw your picture on Charlotte's Instagram page. I'd like you to work for us. I'd like you to draw pictures for our magazine. Can you help us? Please send me a message. Dave Perkins.---

Marty was so surprised, and very happy.

I just wanted to do something nice for a stranger, he thought. *And now, maybe I can work as an artist and quit the bakery!*

4. THE RABBIT

Max was a taxi driver in Boston. Most days he drove out to Logan International Airport and waited for people who arrived in the USA from other countries. On a very cold January night a young woman walked up to his taxi. She had big bags. She was carrying a young boy and pushing a luggage trolley. She looked very small and very tired.

Max jumped out of his taxi. He took the bags from the luggage trolley.

"Where do you want to go?" he asked.

The young woman said "Cambridge."

Where in Cambridge? thought Max. Then he thought, *It's OK. When we get to Cambridge, I will ask her again.*

The young woman climbed into the back seat of the taxi with the little boy. He was holding a blue toy rabbit.

"How much will it cost to go to Cambridge?" asked the young woman.

"About thirty-five to forty dollars," said Max.

The young woman looked in her purse. "Uh. I think I have enough money. My husband said 'I will meet you at the airport', but he didn't come. I called him, but he didn't answer his phone. So I sent him a text message. I wrote 'we are coming by taxi'. I hope he got the message."

Max looked at her. *She is going to cry,* he thought.

"It's OK, lady," he said. "Let's go."

He watched the woman and the boy in his rear mirror. The boy was asleep. He was holding the rabbit tightly. The woman was half asleep. When they got to Cambridge, Max said loudly. "What's the address?"

"The graduate student apartments on Salton Street. It's a big, tall building on a corner."

When Max stopped the taxi outside the building, a young man was standing outside. He ran to the car and looked inside. He opened the back door. "I am so sorry! I got the day wrong! The time difference! Then I left my phone in the library! I just found it. Let me take Ken."

He reached into the car and lifted the little boy out of the car.

Max took the woman's bags and put them on the pavement.

The young man was still talking very loudly. The young woman climbed out of the taxi and gave Max $40. "It is enough?" she asked.

"Yes," said Max. "It's fine."

She smiled at Max. "Thank you. You are very kind."

Max drove away.

The next day was cold, but it was sunny. Max cleaned his taxi before he started driving. On the backseat he found the blue rabbit.

Oh, no! I think the rabbit is that little boy's favourite toy! Maybe he can't sleep without it!

Max drove to the big apartment building. He parked his taxi and went inside. He looked at the names on the mailboxes. There were more than 50 mailboxes.

What am I going to do? I know the little boy's name is Ken. And I think maybe the young woman was Japanese. The tags on the bags said JAL. I must ask someone.

A tall African man came down the stairs and looked at his mailbox.

"Excuse me," said Max. "Can you help me?"

"How can I help you?" asked the man.

"I am looking for a young woman who lives in this building. Maybe her husband is a student. Maybe she is Japanese. They have a son called Ken."

The man laughed. "I want to help you. But this apartment building is for married students. Many small children live here. Many of the people who live here are from Asia. I don't know everyone."

"Oh, dear," said Max. "What can I do?"

"I don't know," said the man. "You need more information. But good luck!" He put his letters in his pocket and walked away.

Max went back to his taxi. *Maybe I should give up.*

Then he had an idea. *People who live in apartment buildings take their children to the park! I will go and look in the parks near here.*

He looked on his GPS and saw that there were three parks in the area. He locked the car doors and started walking. He was carrying the blue rabbit.

Max walked all around a big park. There were many parents with children. The children were running and playing on the swings and slides. He looked everywhere but he could not see the young woman and the little boy.

He went to the next park. It seemed to be a place for older people. There were a few children, but he didn't see Ken.

Max was tired and he was worried. *I should be working.*

He went to the last park. It was very small. There were seats and paths. Some people were riding bikes. Suddenly he saw the young woman and Ken. Ken was in a pushchair. His mother was sitting on a bench. She was holding the handle of the pushchair, but her head was down. Max walked towards them. The woman was asleep. Ken was asleep too. *He has been crying,* thought Max.

Very quietly, Max put the rabbit into the little boy's hands. He woke a little. "Bunny!" he said. He smiled. He held the toy tightly and went back to sleep. Max smiled as he walked away.

5. IT'S WHAT WE DO IN THE COUNTRY

Oscar lived in a big city. He lived alone in a small apartment. He worked from home for a computer company.

He didn't go out. Every week he ordered his food from a big supermarket. The supermarket delivered the food to his house.

He bought his clothes and everything else he needed on the Internet.

He didn't have friends. His family lived in another city and he hadn't talked to them for a long time. He never saw his neighbours.

Every day he worked on his computer near the window. He watched the people and cars and buses, far below his apartment.

Oscar liked his life. *I don't like people. I don't like talking and laughing and parties. I hate noise. My life is perfect for me,* he thought.

One morning in February, Oscar ate breakfast and sat down at his computer with a big cup of coffee.

He looked at the date. February 11th.

It's my birthday, he thought.

He looked at his email inbox. There were messages from his mother, his sister and a cousin. He didn't open them.

Oscar's birthday was not a good day. Another email was from the company he worked for. It was closing down! At the end of February, Oscar would have no job.

Then he heard the doorbell. *It must be those clothes I ordered online,* he thought. *They came quickly. I expected them to come next week.*

He went to the door and opened it. Oscar was surprised. It was the manager of the apartment building.

"Good morning," he said. "I am sorry, but I have bad news for you."

He gave Oscar a letter and went away.

Oscar went back to his living room and opened the letter.

---*This apartment building will be pulled down. You have to leave the apartment by the end of March.*---

Oscar did no work that day. He looked at his computer for a long time.

My perfect life is finished. I have to change everything - my job, my apartment.... Then he had an idea. *I have a lot of money in the bank. I can do something different. What would I like to do? I want to live in a very quiet place with no people. I want to live alone. Maybe I could be a farmer? But I don't like animals. Maybe I could be a fruit farmer? Trees are quiet, and they don't talk.*

Three days later, Oscar bought a very small farm in Oregon. It was 20 miles from the nearest town. It was a cherry farm. *I don't know anything about growing cherries, but I can learn from the Internet.*

Oscar bought a car. He packed up his computers and his clothes and drove to Oregon to start his new life.

The little farm was very pretty. There was a long driveway from the road. The house was small and old, but Oscar liked it.

But country life was very difficult for Oscar. He had always lived in a city. The supermarket in the nearest town did not do home deliveries. Oscar had to drive to town and go shopping. His new car was good for the city but it was not good for country roads. The Internet connection was not good. Sometimes Oscar could connect to the Internet, and sometimes he couldn't. This made him very angry.

The worst thing was the people! They were so friendly! When he arrived at his farm, cars drove up to the house. The people knocked on the door. They called to him. Oscar didn't answer. They left welcome gifts of cookies and pies. They left notes inviting him to a welcome party, a BBQ and the school festival.

When he drove to town, everyone he passed waved to him. The people in the gas station and the supermarket wanted to talk to him. People offered to help him with his farm. Oscar hated it. He didn't answer them.

At the end of March, the cherry blossoms came. His trees were so beautiful. When his Internet was working, Oscar studied hard. He thought he knew everything about being a cherry farmer.

Then, the first week in April, there was a terrible storm. The wind was very strong and it rained and rained. Trees fell down and Oscar could not drive his car down to the road. He had no electricity. His cherry trees did not look beautiful. All the blossoms had blown away in the wind. Then the wind took half the roof off his house! The rain was coming into the house. Oscar tried to cover his computer with a blanket. He was cold and very sad.

I used all my money to come here!! I have lost everything, he thought. He put on a raincoat and wrapped a wet blanket around himself. Suddenly, for the first time, Oscar felt lonely.

Finally, the wind and rain stopped.

It was cold and very quiet *I don't like silence anymore,* he thought.

Suddenly, there was a lot of noise outside his house. The man from the gas station was there with a big truck. There were small trucks and a tractor too. About 20 people were talking, laughing and shouting.

They were taking big sheets of plastic and ladders from the trucks. The tractor was pulling the trees away from his driveway.

Other men were climbing onto his roof with the sheets of plastic. They were covering the holes. Some women with small children came into the house. They were carrying a camping stove and boxes of food. They went into Oscar's kitchen, and after a while, he could smell coffee. Oscar could not believe it.

Why are these people doing this for me? I was so unfriendly. I was very rude. Why are they so kind?

He sat and watched. In a very short time, everything was finished. The trees were gone from the driveway. The hole in the roof was closed. Everyone crowded into the house. There was delicious food on the table. There was coffee and beer.

Everyone was talking. It was a party!

Finally, Oscar could say something. "Thank you! Thank you! I was so rude and unfriendly. Why did you come and help me so much?"

One of the older men smiled. "It was a bad storm and you had bad luck. Of course we helped you. It's what we do in the country."

THANK YOU

Thank you for reading The Kindness of Strangers. We hope you enjoyed it. (Word count: 4,245)

If you would like to read more graded readers, please visit our website http://www.italkyoutalk.com

Other Level 2 graded readers include
Adventure in Rome
Andre's Dream
A Passion for Music
Christmas Tales
Danger in Seattle
Don't Come Back
Finders Keepers…
John Sees a Murder
Marcy's Bakery
Men's Konkatsu Tales
Message in a Bottle
Murder on Whale Island
Salaryman Secrets!
Stories for Halloween
The Perfect Wedding
The House in the Forest
The School on Bolt Street
Train Travel

ABOUT THE AUTHOR

I Talk You Talk Press is an award-winning Japan-based publisher of language textbooks, graded readers and language learning/teaching resources.

Our team is made up of highly experienced language teachers and translators, who have all studied at least one additional language to an advanced level.

This experience enables us to design our materials from the perspective of both the teacher and the learner. We consult with both teachers and language learners when designing our textbooks and graded readers, and test our materials extensively in the classroom before publication.

We are a fast-growing press, and currently publish graded readers for learners of English. We publish new graded readers monthly.

The Kindness of Strangers